YOUR KNOWLEDGE HAS VALUE

- We will publish your bachelor's and master's thesis, essays and papers

- Your own eBook and book - sold worldwide in all relevant shops

- Earn money with each sale

Upload your text at www.GRIN.com
and publish for free

Bibliographic information published by the German National Library:

The German National Library lists this publication in the National Bibliography; detailed bibliographic data are available on the Internet at http://dnb.dnb.de .

This book is copyright material and must not be copied, reproduced, transferred, distributed, leased, licensed or publicly performed or used in any way except as specifically permitted in writing by the publishers, as allowed under the terms and conditions under which it was purchased or as strictly permitted by applicable copyright law. Any unauthorized distribution or use of this text may be a direct infringement of the author s and publisher s rights and those responsible may be liable in law accordingly.

Imprint:

Copyright © 2018 GRIN Verlag
Print and binding: Books on Demand GmbH, Norderstedt Germany
ISBN: 9783668674264

This book at GRIN:

https://www.grin.com/document/418490

Laura Durguti

"Unspeakable Thoughts, Unspoken". The Problem of Communicating Painful Past Experiences in Toni Morrison's "Beloved"

GRIN Verlag

GRIN - Your knowledge has value

Since its foundation in 1998, GRIN has specialized in publishing academic texts by students, college teachers and other academics as e-book and printed book. The website www.grin.com is an ideal platform for presenting term papers, final papers, scientific essays, dissertations and specialist books.

Visit us on the internet:

http://www.grin.com/

http://www.facebook.com/grincom

http://www.twitter.com/grin_com

ET: Toni Morrison's *Beloved*
Autumn 2017

Laura Durguti

8.01.18

"Unspeakable Thoughts, Unspoken"[1]
The Problem of Communicating Painful Past Experiences in *Beloved*

In the fragmented novel *Beloved* Toni Morrison plunges the reader in the middle of 1873, eight years after the end of the Civil War. The readers discover the former black slaves' attempt to fight their haunting memories on the one hand and to find their own language to talk about their painful past on the other. The protagonists of the novel know that healing from the painful past is the key to a better future. Therefor, one of the ways to evacuate the painful past is to talk about it in order to get over it. However, due to their profound trauma the characters of the novel find their "speech blocked" (Wyatt 476) impossible to express their past experiences. Through the use of circumlocutions, the tropes, the songs, the dancing, the crying and the fragmentation of the novel, Morrison demonstrates that storytelling in *Beloved* is an important and a problematic issue thus drawing attention to the problem of speaking about things that are difficult or even impossible to communicate.

 Even if Sethe is one of the figures to tell her past stories in a narrative way, the use of circumlocutions serves as an indicator of her difficulty to communicate her past events. Firstly, when Sethe tries to tell the killing of Beloved to Paul D, she is making constant circular movements, which reflect her storytelling that is told in circumlocutions. There is a parallelism between her body's movements "[s]he was spinning. Round and round the room." (187), and between her storytelling "[c]ircling, circling, now she was gnawing something else instead of getting to the point"(191). The

---

[1] Morrison, Toni. *Beloved*, p. 235.

fact that Sethe is turning around the room shows that she does not feel well when she has to talk about her daughter's death. Moreover, talking about the killing is even harder because she tries to escape from it by talking about something else. Furthermore, the description of Beloved's killing takes six pages to be told (187-193). During these six pages, Sethe's storytelling is filled with circumlocutions, stream of consciousness, euphemism, and gaps. On page 190 (line beginning with: "I did it. I got us all out [...] ending with "I was that wide.") Sethe plunges in a stream of consciousness where her thoughts and feelings are depicted and they leave no place to objective interruptions. The sentences are short, punctuated and with some ungrammatical constructions. Moreover, while telling her story Sethe uses euphemisms, which can be seen on page 192 "[...] over there where no one could hurt them. Over there. Outside this place, where they would be safe" and on page 193 "I stopped him, [...]. I took and put my babies where they'd be safe." The use of euphemism shows that according to Sethe death means the end of slavery, and the end of slavery means safety. Killing her baby was the only way for Sethe to keep her children free. Moreover, when Sethe says that she "stopped [schoolteacher]", she shows that killing was the only way to stop slavery. Grillo Mirkut Giulia notes "[that] you need to die to beat the system" (75). When Sethe finally reaches to the main point of the story, she has difficulties to verbalize the act. Jean Wyatt writes that "[Sethe] finds [her] speech blocked [...] a gap remains at the heart of the story which the omniscient narrator subsequently fills in" (476). By doing so, Sethe is placing herself in a position of avoidance and evasion. The narrator fills the gap and describes the killing of the crawling-already? girl as:

> Simple: she was squatting in the garden and when she saw them coming and recognized schoolteacher's hat, she heard wings. Little hummingbirds stuck their needle beaks right through her headcloth into her hair and beat their wings. And if she thought anything it was No. No. Nono. Nonono. Simple." (192)

This quote demonstrates in a metaphorical way Sethe's attempt to kill herself and her children in order to prevent schoolteacher to re-enslave them. For instance, "she heard wings" can be seen as an immediate flashback in Sethe's head, where she remembers her life as a slave. "Needle beaks", which penetrate Sethe's head show that she immediately reminds the way schoolteacher abused and mistreated her. She has the picture of her mistreatment stuck in her head. Thus, her mind is yelling "No. Nono. Nonono", she knows that she does not want her children to experience the same mistreatment. Therefore, she simply decides, without reflecting, to kill them. The repetition of the word "simple" shows that it was an evidence for her; to kill them meant to free them. Later in the novel Sethe continues to explain her act by saying that "[…] if I hadn't killed her she would have died and that is something I could not bear to happen to her" (236). Once again, with the word "killing" Sethe means putting her children in a safe place, because she simply could not allow her children to experience slavery. Grillo mirkut argues that "[t]his interpretation allows the reader to understand (at least partly) the murder (76). Finally, the use of circumlocutions, euphemisms, stream of consciousness and gaps show the difficulty of Sethe to convey poignant meanings. Sethe is one of the characters in *Beloved* that finds herself in a condition of circling because she can neither confront nor communicate her painful story. Florian Bast points out in his article that characters in *Beloved* are "[…] employing perpetual troping to cognize the traumatic event." (Bast 1079). In my view, tropes are instead reinforcing character's troubles of communication about their terrible past events.

Secondly, there is another interesting passage that indicates well Sethe's problem of communicating her past events. For instance, she never says to Paul D that she was beaten; in the passage on pages 18-20 she talks in circumlocutions and gaps as well. While Paul asks her more information about the tree, there are gaps, which are filled by the omniscient narrator, who describes what Sethe does and how she avoids answering. Paul D (the reader as well) must find it out by himself over the space of three pages (18-20). Sethe circumvents the details of the event. Instead she calls the scar of her back, which is left by whipping, a "chokecherry tree", as Amy Denver said it to her (18). The imagery and the metaphor of the tree in Sethe's back not only hide the violence of the event but it also confuses Paul D. When he tries to learn more about it, Sethe talks in circumlocutions and she avoids mentioning directly the mistreatment she experienced; she shifts from the tree on her back to her breasts full with milk. She now prefers to focus on her maternal side. She puts herself in a position of a nurse, because what hurt Sethe the most, is the fact that schoolteacher took her milk (19), thus depriving her from her mother role. It is this fact that destroyed Sethe more than the scars on her back. Even when Paul D finally finds out that schoolteacher's nephews had beaten Sethe, she never affirms it directly. Instead she focuses more on the loss of her milk:

> "They used cowhide on you?"
> "And they took my milk."
> "They beat you and you was pregnant?"
> "And they took my milk." (20)

Through this quotation Sethe affirms that she was beaten indirectly throughout the conjunction "and". The conjunction shows that she agrees that she was beaten but there was a bigger loss, which is the fact that they took her milk. The repetitions of the sentence "[a]nd they took my milk" points out the fact how tormented Sethe was by the deprivation of her role as a mother. Schoolteacher deprived her as well from her exclusive bond with her crawling already? girl, which is breastfeeding. Once again this passage demonstrates Sethe's impossibility to convey her experiences as a slave.

One of the ways that communities find expression in *Beloved* is through song. Firstly, Baby Suggs' ceremonies are centred around song and dance. For instance, Baby

Suggs is the preacher of the black community; she leads them to an open place called the Clearing. However, she knows that the community has difficulties to evoke their past experiences. Therefore, instead of asking them to express themselves in a narrative way, she helps them to evacuate through singing, dancing, laughing and crying. "It started that way: laughing children, dancing men, crying women and then it got mixed up" (103). Hence, Baby Suggs is helping her community to heal themselves, by going back to their roots in order to let her community understand that they have ancestors and an identity. Nonetheless, the fact that Baby Suggs has invented a new mass ceremony demonstrates that her community is stained with past scars that need to be healed. It also demonstrates that there are some experiences that are simply impossible to communicate. Therefore, they are healing themselves from distasteful past events that are difficult to be told in a narrative way.

Secondly, Paul D. hardly ever talks about his painful past. He has difficulties to communicate his experiences as a slave. Instead of talking about it, he chooses to sing:

> Little rice, little bean,
> No meat in between,
> Hard work ain't easy,
> Dry bread ain't greasy.

This poem sang by Paul D masks suffering through the beauty of rhymes, rhythm, and melody. In order to focus on the meaning that the poem conveys, Paul D gives the reader the possibility to focus on the poetic part such as the very regular tetrameter and the couplet rhymes. There is also a consonance of the sound "I" in "bean" and "between". Thus, by singing it is easier for Paul D to evoke his past, because he hides behind the music the fact that he and other slaves had to work hard and they got almost no food in return. Moreover, singing is linked to the community moments, which allow him to go back to his roots.

Furthermore, there is a passage where Paul D makes an effort to tell to Sethe one specific past experience (85-86). It is while Paul D was chained, had a bit in his mouth and was confronted with a free rooster (86). The free animal made Paul D realize that he was treated worse than animals. The bit in his mouth took away his human characteristic, which is that of speaking. This experience is painful and shameful that Paul D has difficulties to communicate it. This difficulty of communication is shown through his narration. While he talks about it, his sentences are short, incomplete and followed with ellipsis "Mister, he looked so . . . free [...] he was still king and I was . . ." (86). The ellipses mark his inability to evoke the way he felt during his life as a slave. He is also making body movements "Paul D stopped and squeezed his left hand with his right. He held it that way long enough for it and the world to quiet down and let him go on."(86). This quotation strongly suggests that Paul D is shivering during the narration. The shivering of his hands mirror the trauma that slave life has caused to Paul D. The fact that he needs to stop his narration in order to calm down shows the traumatic impact of the experience on Paul D. Thus, this trauma is driving attention to the problem of speaking about things that are difficult or even impossible to express. Sethe, who listens to Paul D remarks it and makes him stop by caressing his knee. This touch stops Paul D from his narration "[...] her fingers on his knee [...] stopped him. Just as well. Just as well" (86). Sethe, did not only stopped him but also relieved him from bringing back the heavy weight of the painful past. This relief is seen through the repetition of the sentence "[j]ust as well". Finally, Paul D will leave his story untold, which demonstrates the impossibility to communicate it.

Additionally, there is another characteristic that demonstrates Paul D's difficulties to express his experiences; it is the invention of the tobacco tin. He says that he replaced his heart through the tin, where he keeps painful memories locked. The fact that he locks his memories highlights his inability to communicate them. The tin demonstrates as well that Paul D needs to repress his memories in order to protect himself and to survive. Otherwise, the protagonist knows that trying to communicate and to confront the atrocities of slavery can overwhelm a person, as happens to Halle, who goes mad (other slaves as well). Thus, the tobacco tin helps Paul D to keep a distance with his traumatic events.

Last but not least, we see that characters must use different tropes while they tell their events. In my view, there can be two different interpretations of the use of the tropes in the novel. On the one hand, the former slaves use tropes in order to hide the suffering and to make their past scars bearable to be told. On the other hand, the use of tropes, which beautifies the mistreatments, points out the fact that white people pretended to be naïve and refused to admit the miserable treatment they were making on slaves. Furthermore, they did it in order to have a clear conscience. Therefore, Morrison shows how the definers also white people abused definitions, such as defining the places where slaves worked hard as "sweet home". The abuse is shown through Paul D, who points out that "it wasn't sweet and it sure wasn't home" (16).

The fragmented form of the novel forces the reader to reconstruct the traumatic story, thus accentuating the tragedy of the character's situation. Indeed, the idea of reconstruction is within and without the text. In the story of the novel, the former black slaves try, as hard as they can, to reconstruct their past, to get over it in order to create a sound future. The reconstruction is harder since their memories are vague, mixed, fragmented and sometimes even lost. The hardest part of it is that every inch of their memory brings them pain. In the novel Morrison underlines this when Amy Denver says "[a]nything dead coming back to life hurts" (42) / "More it hurt more better it is. Can't nothing heal without pain [...]" (92). The reader on the other side gets a fragmented story, which forces him to have an active reading, to reconstruct it, and that is not an easy task. The author masterfully shifts the tenses of storytelling, using the past, the present and the future. Moreover, Morrison changes as well the narration of the novel, which switches from the first-person narrator to the third person; and from the limited narration to the omniscient narration. She does all of this without preventing the reader or without giving any indications for it.

Furthermore, the play with language, with the form, and with the fragmentation not only makes the structure of the novel complex and sophisticated but it indicates as well the difficulty to convey past traumas. Cynthia Dobbs argues that the reason Morrison never gives the whole story is because of "the inability of any vocabulary to contain certain experiences" (qtd in Grillo Mirkut 67). I would add that the fragmentation of the novel mirrors character's difficulties to express their terrible past. Therefore, in the absence of speaking subjects, the author uses body language. For instance – as showed earlier in this essay – while characters try to talk about their past, their bodies are mirroring the discomfort of their experiences. Indeed, Sethe makes circular movements around the room while she tries to talk about her past experiences; Paul D's hands shiver; Baby Suggs and all the community members sing, dance, laugh, and cry because they cannot talk about what happened to them. They try to heal themselves, in different ways in order to get over their past traumas.

To conclude, the novel demonstrates the post-traumatic shock of former black slaves. The author shows that freeing oneself from slavery was only a first step toward freedom. The hard work, the violence, the abuse, the rape (and all other acts of mistreatment) have marked the slave's life through physical and psychological scars. Each of the slaves has lived different horrible experiences, thus each of them tries to find out a way to get over it, in order to construct a future. Nevertheless, going back to the painful past memory is the hardest task to do; it is like a hurricane that comes and destroys everything, leaving behind only destruction and pain. Although it hurts, the former slaves try to find the courage to confront it, because it is only by beating the past that they could live freely in the present. Thus, Morrison demonstrates how the characters of her novel struggle while they try to convey their past stories. Indeed, the narration of character's past events goes hand in hand with tropes such as circumlocutions, metaphors, euphemisms, stream of consciousness, gaps etc. The narration is followed as well with the body movements; each time the characters talk about their past, they are in constant movements. Moreover, when past experiences are impossible to convey some characters sing, in order to make the traumatic events poetic thus masking its suffering through music. Other community members never talk about their past. It is exactly in this way that Morrison points out how problematic the theme of storytelling is. The use of tropes, music, dance, body movements and all the other ways of expression demonstrate the problem of talking about things that are difficult some even impossible to communicate.

Works cited

Bast, Florian. "Reading Red: the Troping of Trauma in Toni Morrison's Beloved." Ed. Callallo. Vol. 34(4), 2011. 1069-1086.

Grillo Mikrut, Giulia. "You your best thing, Sethe. You are: African American Maternal Experience in Toni Morrison's Beloved." *Living Language Living Memory: essays on the Works of Toni Morrison*. Ed. W Shands Kerstin & Grillo Mikrut Giulia. Sweden: Södertörns högskola, 2014. 67-83.

Morrison, Toni. *Beloved*. London: Vintage, 2005.

Wyatt, Jean. "Giving Body to the Word: The Maternal Symbolic in Toni Morrison's *Beloved*." Ed. PMLA. Vol. 108(3). 1993. 474-488.

Bibliography

Kella, Elizabeth. Beloved Communities. Solidarity and Difference in Fiction by Michael Ondaatje, Toni Morrison, and Joy Kogawa. Edsbruk: Akademitryck, 2000.

Khawaya, Mabel et al. "Toni Morrison's *Beloved*." Ed. The Teaching of Literature. Vol. 112, n° 1. 1997. 115-118.

YOUR KNOWLEDGE HAS VALUE

- We will publish your bachelor's and master's thesis, essays and papers

- Your own eBook and book - sold worldwide in all relevant shops

- Earn money with each sale

Upload your text at www.GRIN.com
and publish for free